My Search of
ORDER

Isaac Delagrue

ISBN 978-1-64191-739-1 (paperback)
ISBN 978-1-64191-740-7 (digital)

Copyright © 2018 by Isaac Delagrue

All rights reserved. No part of this publication may be reproduced, distributed, or transmitted in any form or by any means, including photocopying, recording, or other electronic or mechanical methods without the prior written permission of the publisher. For permission requests, solicit the publisher via the address below.

Christian Faith Publishing, Inc.
832 Park Avenue
Meadville, PA 16335
www.christianfaithpublishing.com

Printed in the United States of America

Introduction

I had made no plan as I passed from the womb in the character I would be. In imagining, so I envisioned a good-natured chap I should be. Not shall I recall in here and there I have been. Many a splendid life I have lived in; so challenged I've been from the start. To apply limitation or boundaries alike were so not to be within me. For if I ride the swiftest horse through the rain and puddles, a tree I would surely be not.

I am being not able to stay a course or stand idly by. When the wind shifts, I hear my name, waning my soul urged to soar. To find joy in my own self's amazement, a kindling to start a warmth's fire. Then be as I am shall greatly achieve the moment they be at hand.

Times will change; habits form in the flower shall bloom. Will not I invite the occasions that harbor my vessel near sin. My sloop shall tow not adventure, nor shall it be left to the wake. May the wind blow in true moderation and the sails to not even a score. What will become a crew then a cast will share harmonies work, side by side.

The making of all that grow tattles and tales of legends they've been born. Which matters most of where we've been is a telling accurately. In all the poise repeating exactly as first told.

Down on through the ages followed, one after another, a book paused in preparation—centuries apart. To choose by indignation many years from now prevent the truth be told of one man's exploits. Be a saint, a sinner, not divested of the self. When one comes up to a wall, do you leap or climb, tunnel or fall? If stories make a book, be it fiction, be it truth.

The Red Coats

Into the night I must
Make my distance count
In the speed of lightning, something just as quick
Future breaths depend on this
As I shall stake my life
It has been three years I left my happy home
The mother and the father which raised me as their own
Spoke to me one night, suggesting that the military
Could be my way of life
After swearing to the king my allegiance
The troops boarded a ship
For the British Colonies in America,
somewhere across the ocean, seas
I never would have dreamt, my life's years be spent
Soldiering through the Boston Streets, rebellion in the air
Every street and corner, suspicion with cold stares
Not of a trusting nature nor nurturing with the care
Anger below the surface, stirring in the place
Of what could have been community
Instead of mere distrust, resentment

I once upon an afternoon patrolling the country side
Came upon a farm just over the next hill
I assumed a farmer having daughters well of age
I strolled clear of the patrol, closer to the well
Asking would she draw me water
"Do it for yourself," she bellowed
Absence of a smile or grin
She climbed the steps to the porch, forward toward the door

If closed much harder, would the hinges hold
My doubts of subtlety arose
Having looked over her shoulder
For reasons, I don't know
Though thought I much later on

A day or two later, again on a patrol
I made a point to wander
Closer to the farm and home
Of one attractive maiden
I have failed yet to impress
My efforts did seem stranded
A strong hint of hopelessness

On this very day, expressed sentiments a must
She did draw water for me, called me an invader
Asking why don't I return
I wondered why I hadn't
Back from where and which I came
I searched my soul a moment, in hope an epiphany
We onward with an argument, a discussion did ensue
Later in the moment, found myself divided
Not very self-assured
Very well from my comrades
I rushed and ran, until I could no more
A search made high and low
Away from quarters or a late return
Would cause me pain and suffering
Humiliation I have known
Of which I now deserved for my very own

Darkness was well upon me to overcome me shortly
As I approached the town
Not much more a village

Where billeting was found
Control of all homes was needed
For our lodging was required
People in the streets, no place to lay their heads
No house to call their own, as they froze onto the streets
Somehow, this seemed not right
Familiar in some ways

I listened for a minute, standing at the door
The evening meal had started
I could hear the voices clear
Some recognized, some not
Now among the missing, I had caused myself
As I truly had been afar
Do I enter and accept, the fate I measured for
Should I simply flee
Knowing if caught, what awaited me
Would be a bitter, tragic shortcoming
To what until now has been my life, you see

An insurmountable restless moment
Had gripped upon my soul
The obstructed point of view
Was there, right from wrong
In times, similar to this
Could I be imagining
This to be a sort of dream
One I fear to wake up from
I want to run and scream

The echoes came to me, from inside my head
I could not bear it, knowing I not able
To endure the painful challenge
The thought not a reward

For getting side tracked, so far down the road
Late to understand, what I did and did not do
Circumstance dictated nothing to be new
I must get out of view
A dire possibility awaited me if not
I walked a pace in double quick
To the edge of town, I knew
I came up to a bridge
That would be guarded soon
Until the morning hour, well after the sun rise
If I cross this moment, they'll be no turning back

I shall need to seek refuge before the snow does fall again
For now, I need to cross the bridge
My footsteps to be gone
It burns a picture in my head
Will shortly grows to ache
Crossing over into, where I'd never been
If I hadn't stopped at the farm and let the maiden be
All that now seems happenstance
Could fade into the setting sun
Each wisp would touch vapor then in turn to wind

No! I must clear my head
Must not misplace mind, good sense
The adventure has begun, the journey now must start
Better late than never, my vision now will be
The chance meeting of a maiden and myself
Will she greet me with a smile?
For my heaven and hell are colliding
Beneath the near full moon
I will have walked for hours seemingly
Afore the morning light
I must travel off the road

Staying off the trail
Concealment of my footsteps
Seemed quite proper at the time
After walking knee, deep in the snow
Without benefit of watch
I chanced to see a chimney's smoke
Further off the road, down a ragged trail
To where my journey leads, I only hope I have
Found my way to paradise after leaving misery

There be no chance of drawing attention at this hour
I searched for something shelter like
Until I heard, a barking dog
Into the springhouse I did slide
Hardly was an opening to allow myself inside
I laid down in the darkness as close as I felt dry
So be it, God, please look upon me
favorably, I know not what to do
At least until the morning, do I come or go
Amen

Waiting for the morning became a mystery
Of what time it may, I can determine not
In the darkness and the cold
As in a crypt, I anticipate
My freedom from the cold
I drift back into slumber in hopes I do awake

The spots where light may travel have
allowed a stream to me
Time for eyes adjustment was fortunately foreseen
I now can hear the footsteps breaking upon the frozen snow
I traverse what is mud to the driest of the corners
In my splendid solitude

Someone has arrived, for better or the worst
I know not the outcome
God, forgive me for all I've done
Notwithstanding of my own prayer
I hold my breath, the door begins to creak
She sees my shadow, as the maiden
turns she looks upon my face
"Goodness gracious!" in a scolding tone
"What in God's name are ya doing here?"
Some moments later, my story had been told
"The first thing we must do," she says
"Is get you some dryer clothes"
The rest is unexplainable, I could hear the changing tone
In the midst of all the turmoil a level head prevailed
She would sneak me into the cellar of the house
I would be less likely to be found
The rest all in good of its own will surely come to life
Footsteps in the snow would betray us in good time
For now, the ravenous was longing for my needs
The thought of food escaping or of all nourishment
Had eluded to my safety
For in the darkness travelled have brought me here to you
I rehearsed not once but twice
My reasons that I knew
Brought me to the wilderness, in a search of you

"C'mon," she beckoned with her hand waving
Toward an outside door, with steps through the foundation
I had to crouch once more
She closed the door behind me I settled
out, then into a darkness
I was a pawn of my own chess game hiding on the board
I trust she possessed the skills
To amicably pull it off

Again, I wait in darkness as again my long lost friend
I can hear the weight of hooves as they cross the ground
Among the random of the wagons, I do hear voices now
Some are giving orders then acknowledged shouts
One had sounded close and moving toward the door
For an instance, the path to daylight clear
Something had been dropped
Appeared a cloth bag full of fruit and bread
My mouth thus started watering
The feast had now begun
I ate what I could, and then I hunkered down

The maiden did seem true to me
For her I must account
To keep our secret secretly
Above her I no doubt
About midday another bag dropped through the door
Full of farmers clothes, a note attached inside
Change into these clothes, place yours in the bag
Please stay out of sight
I obliged to her request in a short matter of my time
The afternoon was lengthy, I occupied my mind
Writing simply in the mind's tablet,
the order of the day's events
I could not have imagined this, not with all the zest
To become stranded on an island, all so far from home
In a country I knew nothing of, in the cellar of a house
How could things be better, how could they be worse

As evening approached so quietly
The absence of a mouse
I was not clear to see the sun
It had slowly eked its way, then passed over the house
My hunger it had grown, my restlessness pursued me

Into the darkness hours I admit
I was utmost grateful for protection
I had not seen her face to face, for most of the first day
I must find the words to thank the maiden
As she took my interest to heart, for her very own

With evening came more darkness
I could hear footsteps coming near
The door cracked open slightly
A bag with food and blankets, another note attached
Dropped on through the opening
With this I heard her scurry back across the yard
I waited for her to stop, I opened up the bag
I ate, for was my first concern
Some bread and fruit and pie
I made a bed of blankets, but the note thought I
Will have to wait till morning, I haven't any light
So down my head and closed my eyes
Until morning my Lord, thank you
Amen, goodnight

The morning came, seemed early
Made no never mind
I stretched my legs and arms laying on my back
Some time it had been since I'd straightened up to stand
As oddly as it sounds I was living under ground
Don't mistake me presumptuous
On every front, I'm grateful
Appreciate the kindness, I should read the note
Crawling on my knees, though cold and stiff they be
I need just enough of daylight
In hope that I can read

It started out describing family
Father and Mother loyalist to the Crown
I found this some disheartening
If I were to be discovered, located, or found
There would be no doubt the sanctions
The end would come to everything
For sure it would come soon
A line of soldiers aiming directly at my heart
From not too great a distance
My eyes covered assuredly
Not lasting long the pain
Into the ground I'd slumber
The end to all my days
I twitched then shivered, wiped my aching head
I continued to read on
She explained that she sought liberty
As much to any cost
Divided from her parents
Often feeling lost
You know that when the thaw comes
Look for you they must
You must stay alert during day light hours
Quiet while the dark
If at all detected, you'll be shot on this very sight
If they know the rest
There will be the lot to pay
I will wait a day or two for you to decide
What shall work the best
I have some help some friends
When I am sure, who and what you are
I'll move you not till then

On this day of all, I stayed awake some how
The cold was jerking at me, chill nipping at my heels

Though shielded by the wind
Subjected to the cramps of being curled up like a rope
I caught no glimpse of my young friend
She strolled by several times, the cellar door and I
All of a sudden
Dropped a bag of roast meat, vegetables, and fruit
She avoided easily attaching another note
I sought just to thank her
For the kindness of her heart
Must be her bringing up
The risk she now took daily
Patiently apprised of my situation
Of which now I hide

Darkness arrived for me, a bit early on this night
It took its grip in restlessness
I came upon a want
A desire to stand and walk around
Circulation to my feet and legs
For the pins and needles to subside
I would not make a sound
An hour after supper, a bit before bed time
Another bag of blankets
A scribbled note inside
Again, to wait till morning, there is no light at all
Wrapping up in blankets with my head inside, enthralled
In hopes this way through night

I slept in late this morning, not time to read the note
The one foot of each, three sized men
aiming rifles at my head
Quickly was I awaking to see
Juggled from my bed
They are all three wearing the Red Coats

I am making of the forth
British Rifles I can see
Rushing Bayonets to my face
My hopes have all been dashed
Will not see my parents
Into the cold, cold ground
For everything included, my maiden let me down
I was grateful for the sun, the warmth came upon my face
My hands tied well behind me, no hat was I to wear
To protect my youthful head
I was pushed into a wagon, ample room for me
One soldier in the rear behind me
Two upon the seat
We made our way to the fork in the road
I wondered what if first
Would I be taken into town?
An example would I be made of
That would be different I was sure
I had heard of deserted soldiers, never to be found
I had not given it much thought, up to and until now
My mind began to hurry almost making sound
The wagon began to slow
It stopped and started again
A soldier in the front had dropped down to the ground
Sometime after we turned south we started to go west
In my attempt to ask a question I was shushed to stop
I maintained my silence for longer than I had
For what seemed to me important
Shoved deep in my pants pocket, not a chance to read
A note from my betrayer
Who sent soldiers such as these
Confusion had escaped me, having credited her job
Having gone above her duty
Now, I surely would meet mine

My travelling companions and I had moved of all day
Half-awake I realized from my slumber I awoke
We were straying from the trail, coming off the road
Behind a clump of trees, pine if I dared to guess
The soldiers went behind the clump together
Came out singularly
I had made my getaway, running cross a field
They sought me in pursuit in the wagon they did ride
In minutes, I was captured
They did not understand
One said to the other, he didn't read the note
I begged to see more clearly
Where are your three Red Coats
One says to me defiance in his eyes
Reach into your pocket, kindly read the note
Now he had reminded me I had overslept
I reached into my pocket and pulled the paper free
Unfolded it, began to read

In the morning three soldiers will arrive
Wearing all Red Coats
If you trust me all assuredly
Please do, go with them
They will do you no harm
This was arranged by me
Another day spent in the cellar
You surely would be caught
I heard you rustling
Whenever I walked by

The end of hostilities is nearing
So go where these men go
If you feel the need for liberty
These three will escort you to the winning side

Be grateful for your fortune
If my father or mother had found you
You would be in the cold, cold ground
I am looking forward to seeing you again
On a summer day
Standing in the yard
Not in the cellar way
Until then, my Red Coat
Until then, farewell

The Red Coats

Chapter Two

The wagon pulled for what had seemed
I'll make no never mind, for what could have been
The young lass saved my ever-loving life
I could not believe my eyes, I'll swear
The stack of Bibles high
Awakening to the Red Coats, I was certain
someone was bound to die
Sure, as I about to take my last as mortal breath
While looking toward her eyes
I would have felt a moment or maybe two betrayed
I would have negated any blindfold
Of my last chance, just to peer
Toward my blossomed, farm girl friend
Whom I hardly barely knew at all
Until near the bitterest of ends
I looked up into the heavens as the
wagon came around a bend
I'll not be of worthy, cannot wash from my two hands
The guilt I have portrayed over in my mind
Somehow, I've been rescued, not sure as to why
All the rules in happenstance have shaded each my eyes
Father in Heaven, thank you having shown me the way
Of all elongated possibilities of shouldered you in me
I thank you once again
Amen

The road appeared impassable, just after the bend
Awkward, still to me as seemingly
I found myself, as best to put it
On the other end

*

Miles down road, much further in the route
We three stopped, alongside of the road
I could just remove myself from the wagon's load
The camp and fire made, between the greenest trees
A simple meal of beef and biscuits
not truly much was saved
I chanced a glance at the sunset
I closed my eyes to see
the beauty in the farm girl, I would soon hope to see
The four walls of our own farm house
A family will be
cast in all my daydreams
In all sincerity, I will find her once again
For she led this man to freedom
I mean to thank her yet, from the bottom of my heart.

A Sandy Gated Beach

Here, by the moonlight, a moment hath passed
Her breath taken, one at a time
From across the room I venture
In silence I dare, careful my steps I stagger
Within my means to move
One foot than the other
A woven dream, from off the loom
She, her fragrance only mine
Attributes not final or in a wearied stage
A toss she turns, her hair adjusts
Comes the sweeping of a hand
I sit, then not
For there no chair, a travesty averted
Would shame my one and all
Bruises had by morning time
The sunrise, we will call
Setting on the water, by evening was reasoning
A lifetime, one and all
I will serenade the masses
In mine deliverance
An eagle for a turkey
Comes Thanksgiving Day
A porridge for the lonely heart
Awake have gone to sleep
Will be the blast of winter
Mostly all shall freeze
Spring shall bring the thawing
Slowly, timid though not afraid
From out behind the trees

Alley ways and streets
Over land, some from the sky
From lands have travelled by
A summer in attendance
The roast pig warms the bellies
Friendship smooths the heart that beats
In arms brace nostalgia
Traditions at the gate, further down the road
By day's light comes they still

*

There came no time for wandering; the surge had found us quick. There came a thought of storms before, found no time to reminisce. In a memory tomorrow perhaps in a race too close to call. We'll sit around the fire in hopes of keeping warm to suddenly be dry. In a fashion not of temperament came such a raging force. If I've lived to see the one, I've grown to know them all. I watched as I've been witness to the tides pounding the sea wall. Not in favor of such a drenching, see the town folk scamper for the high ground. Our tiny lots lain so imperfectly, and cottages the like. Almost like the clothes line on a cold and windy morning, but even stronger still. We held out for the best, still trembling in a truly well-built barn further up the hill. Able we were to look down where our house once stood. I had caught a vision as my home went sweeping by. Annoyed by reports the night before, the dangling retorts of what was on its way. Heard it before since I was young, of countless dozen times or more. By a knock on the door, nobody home a warning on its way, was gone. To the next house, then the next. As hardened steel we would make no deal; let the devil come. On our way were not, staying put we were. The rain did come and go it went, only to return again and again though harboring a vagrant's smirk. When the daylight comes and all is clear, we'll get up and do it all over again. A lad when this all started, and an old man I've become. Swept the coast, rubbed and scrubbed, a gathering was held. The day had come, balloons were flung, thus flying all about. Some upstairs floors had swayed and moaned, some houses danced the jig as in just the night before as they were carried away. Unearthed betrayed now came the day into the fray and frackus. Residents took no delight in those were swept away. House and home had been their own, now came time so to lament. Was yours mine when mine was yours, at the bottom of the hill. A pile now has named you seaside property. If I stretched my imagination, only if I would or could beyond my finger's tips. I would never have seen this coming, to my segments of the beach. Rebuilding commenced, in timely from the very start. Complete would hope foreseeing, the coming season's start. Years would come as time did pass, so the story went. What seemingly won't last.

A New Sunrise

Alas, my lass!
The time has come.
No warring times nor beating drums.
Shall give witness in portrayal,
to body's language so betrothed.
In what one thinks, for all to know,
ideas scattered, for the winds to show.
Blustering as agile will,
a remedy sewn, will pose in manner.
Forgiveness will, there always shall,
await an outcome, be it sad.
In our world of sought out peace,
the venture weighs, none in control.
For the future has and shall remain,
none in obstacle, a try in gain.
The depths preserve, for in the hearts,
two do beat as one.
As horizon goes, yet it comes.

A Roadside Stay

Ahoy! We've come to captivate
By image, willed in my extra literary form
To one eye, so the next bequeaths
The pretense all but spent
When the armaments of fury past
Hell hath no fury, such
In concerted requiem,
We pause to raise the glass
Drink not of flavored water
The truest, choicest wines
Tepid by decision, a relegated past
In agreement, nor philosophy
Let begin what has begun
To parch the thirst of every
If not the most find in the able
The wind strives to be still
All is calm tonight
By the simple thought imagined
In a manger shared

I'll not get your goat or a tussle with a sheep
The best the barnyard offers is in his mother's arms
Fast asleep, should be
At last slumber of the we

A Time or Two Ago

From a lifetime, I shall speak
On acronym, each knee of travelled long and far
Mine staff doth hold me steady, standing on a rock
In words an upright song, a melody to change
From one beat to the next
The occasion be the drumroll
With thee shall we speak
My garden grows voluptuous
In the Greek, we'll speak
For no other riches
Were cherished, buried long ago
The lifetime, that I've spoke
With my flowers sewn

A Flickering Course

In as much as we can, with our fingers we point
High on a shelf, things we can't reach
The real and imaginable, that we can't taste
Time and again moments to waste
The tip of a finger
With any good aim
In a moment, all figured
There be no real gain
Blown out again is one in the same
The flickering lights
The wick be too short
A lantern to light
My finger of course
Is steady in reach
The shadow will grow
Until morning does come
The dawning from darkness
Hours since dusk

Alas, My Dears

Alas, my daughters, do not cry
Weep not, for sure am I
Have come home at last
To be at each your side
Have mastered many arts
Of which none were conceived
In spiritual attempts to guide
each of you
To looking deep inside
For in a world of mirth and merriment
The mind and spirit do collide
As two ships often do
when they left behind
The fog is thickest at this moment
and
lips are often dry
Alas, my daughters
I can see into your eyes
Along with and accompanied
By both each of your smiles

Away with the Spoon

As the light of the dawning gives birth, a new day
To the west, passes on as the tides
With each breath anew, in thought will arise
An idea grows to be bright
The edge of the window, let's call it a sill
Through the pane is the view to outside
A storing, a squirrel of thinking to hide
The kitty cat dashes on by
In the briefest of customs, the melee begins
Hark the rider, approached from the north
Of those some, may be better off yet
Let the birds fly, in simplicity's sake
In the greatest triangle of give and take
One will collapse into a straight line
Then bending disfigured as many of will
Past wiggles and worms are so contentious
Dare not, pray tell dream it away
To the surface it floats
Like the dawning's new day
It slivers to vanish
To find its own way

Chosen for You

In peace of mind I find my dreams
Stacked like greeting cards
Those which I have yearned for
Of some, shall go so far
Some which are unopened yet
I've meant to read them all
Worth their weight in good will
Suspended by, and with intent
Messages so timely
In their content is the key
A view the chosen masterpiece
Not to rectify
So not to hang in a museum,
Suspended from a rooftop a ceiling or the like
Perched outdoors for pigeons
Thus in an envelope
Among all required antidotes
Kind words sent in an exchange
Improving all concerns
With a happy birthday
Or
Picturesque the card
Mailed at the last of moments
As have all those gone before

Comes the Day by Morning

Embedded in the strokes of covering the wall,
this one being done, in hurry to the hall

The embers sear through footwear,
a scorching of the feet

Flying down the stairs, one step at the time,
reaching, through the clouds

Onto the road is found

Degree of Dignity

If should, I start to slip and slide
Give points for how I land
More for what is difficult
An eight, a nine, or ten
Should my dismount end abruptly?
One or two, too many twists
The floor came rushing toward me
Right to the sudden stop
Sometime later in the day, I did
Recollect my name
I was left to ponder
If should, I start to slip and slide …

Drama on the Ground

Of and beyond the devil toils
His labors tried and true
If all were to the searching
Shall grasp the hold on you
Our minds a set to lurking
No reason, just despair
One way up,
The downward road
No way down,
The one-way street
Pieces kept in closets
Of clothes were never worn
Crackled dreams reflected
The mirror is explored
In search of the feebled mind
No, not the mighty rogue
His spot now deemed more worthy
Throw him hard and fast
No, drag him 'cause we must
For the, fine print states
Any way we want
Any way we choose
If you seek repentance
From your window seat
Hold your breath, too long in wait
They'll justly bump you at the gate

What Next

She followed me home from school one day
I thought she'd lost her way
Up one lane and down the next
What was I to say

She stayed at the gate a leaning
on the wall was she
Mother then did ask me so
was she a friend to me

I replied in all my wisdom of what
at nine I had to spare
Looked mom in the eye I did
said I was not sure

Go on with you, invite her in your will
If she's like the rest of us
she's in need a meal
so I did what I was told

Out the door went I, I did
at halfway to the gate I waved
Now she knew it was all clear
she came walking in

From the Chill and Wind

To my right I see, as I pass through, the most front of doors
From the cold and wind a fellowship adjourned
A stairwell with attached walled railing
From bottom near to top
To my gaze returning, I standing in the way
To the left I chance to peer
By way of one long deepened sill
She bowed, for two-thirds of the wall
Stopping at the corner, turning
One window being centered
The same distance as the opening
Such left on either side
Coming at last a corner
On the back wall, left to right
An opening starts and runs for five feet
Three feet from the wall
There'll not be another opening
The remainder of the wall

Halfway around the World

To all that is before
Tucked in, with that to come

When it comes unfolded
Hath near, the day been done

With all the zeal of compost
A thought doth come, then gone

The zest with all the rest
With it all, intent means well

A mentioned once a panic
In twice, the afterbirth

Not to save the dragons
Nor preserve the unicorn

An idea could have been
From moments at a loss

A mild meek of many
As the coin is tossed

Listen carefully, can you not hear
The footprints in the sand

A shot heard round the world
The ride of Paul Revere

Legends speak as biblical
corruption of the twist

Stories come unfolded
In some we will adore

Keep it long and deep
The shovel keeps the score

Story One

I'll have kept quiet to myself, being my name and where I've come from. Not I havin' a notion to tossin' around where my whereabouts bin. Am not learned in the proper of gentlemen's ways. Never have and likely won't find nor make time enough for further schoolin' and such. I've a living to make, a head to keep dry, a body to warm, and—most of all for all to hear—a belly yet to fill.

    Not in the habit of sayin', so I will not be starting again. I came by chance upon an empty oaken keg—was made of wood, what else? A strolling I was by the nearby docks, minding my business I was, with nary a wince for a thought. All at once I tried it on for size, just about then I heard. The gent sounded a bit taken angry, further into my spot I hid. It was then I couldn't imagine anything good still to come. Down further I scooched my knees in my chest, my face meeting with both of these. Voices I heard, believin' the two, seemed distant and goin' away. I no longer heard when I thought to get out from where I seemed into strayed. With one foot in and one foot out, in an instant movement came. Back into my barrel I climbed.

    With no notice at all I found myself lifted as to fly, afore I was able to look. Upward seeming endless, a swinging motion downward. The sun having been nearly blocked from view, lower and lower. still yet lower down my barrel and I. Fear had found its juncture seated next to me, so to be uncomfortable, as to wait and see. Time has found me difficult, in a word to my beyond and all is meant to be. My knees grew numb I knelt; as I grew cold I prayed. Evening came, then all got dark; I tell you true, lost I felt I was.

Moments passed in my assurance, to hell I've never been for it did move a certain way. Upsetting I began to feel, hearing voices come once more I stayed deep down inside. For sure, nigh was I able to tell the likes of others, so stayed tight in my place.

I shan't from where I sit see the world in awe. Escapes to me in choices so made out. Soliloquies of turtle doves and "what ifs" in the air in hopes change the hearts of man.

Will a heartbeat here, a drumbeat there upset the appetite? In the thirst of hunger we walk the times to square. The gatherings in markets will exceed in have and done.

My interest staged in diversified scenes to never see. Roaming in and out of alleys, up and down the streets. The days I find my home, I'll make it in so that I have. My castle's highest towers, above a garden not yet grown, a field lost of its green. So high atop a hill my eyes yet to see. I'll not pick the fruit till ready, not dangling from a tree. Be on the carts in markets where they can be seen. There be a time for all left ready in the wake. Let the chimneys belch there in the gracious thanks.

I find myself in wakening, yet the day stays dark. I can sense the breathing of those thought not yet to a wake. In the hull of one great ship, I now fancy me. I'll be chancin' opportunity in a day or here abouts. There be motion in experience as my carriage tilts though doesn't topple; time will hear me out. A home I'll have for now, so to speak I have. There be no clean sheets for my bed or a place to rest my head. As if mine could know the difference of each night where I slept. In motto: I've seen the seeker, so in my seeds be sewn.

I'm given thought to where we are, not in truth I set. My imagination reaches while my arms seem not yet there. There comes of my journey, a musty, moldy smell. Grows that not a likin' will you never hear me tell. A darkened cave I found me in, no sense of the day, be it night. I see not of the sun, nigh gaze unto the stars. If rain shall come, I believe I am to hear. At times while in my quarters I am to feel an echo's breath.

By the journey's end, mad you'll have me be. To survive what seems a one-way trip, no passage had I seen nor had a cost incurred. No expense shall I record, no endeavor could be greater in the absence of what I cannot see,

I been growing hungry, to quench my thirst could serve me well. Whilst I stand to stretch my legs. In turn clear my thoughts while I water down my patience; there seems here time enough. Not understandin' meanin' in words like *virtue*. I hope to get it all, some time while still approaching the new world. Of hearin' tell of schoolin' for old and young alike, regardless of some in other tings not so.

Work is told as plenty, much so to go around. Sounds to me a grand place with both on the ground. Bin not as skilled as others, for now we'll let that be. For being a lad not yet of marrying age. I left in sight the coal mines. They'd soon call my name. My father and his brothers and my, too, cousins living down right by the hill. Mostly they are some bit older than myself; mostly been in mines for more a dozen years. In all what comes to meantime above beneath the rest, if I'll not be again mistaken being bitten by the cold, a chill I can so feel, a frost I cannot see. I find myself not still but in peace, my surroundings besides. There is none in commotion, as far the smooth, long, bumps they rise and fall. Never have I, I truly could not believe to be here in adventure. In this way confined I search the world I know. Calmness comes on slowly, but it comes. It comes.

There is none in need of time or day, in this hole. There is none of all convenience, in no faces I have seen. I sit and stand upon my knees; I bow my head in prayer. I, through my heart, hold no expectin' to a circle being round nigh a box still bin square.

To search the world, none other this place within my oaken wooden chariot would I dare in call my home. If, in simply what comes to matter is what may, to may not be. While up is up, there down be down, it truly can or cannot be.

As a younger lad, a child I was, not yet distinguishing. I could feed myself quite nice with both a fork and spoon. My mouth was to be the target though often was the floor. I'm thinkin' the sun must be upon us is known we cannot see, there is a warmth however welcome, for we are still too be. In the wake forgone a ship, a boat, a floating piece of wood.

I came hampered by a nagging, so in thought it came. So it came more often; I had to send it on its way. It had found the way to cause me uncertain gratitude. Was to come or come and gone. A mystery in the darkness, to wait then we shall see.

Once a young 'un on a pony ride, once around the square, I cried for more and got none. Father often said once more, when the end the end. He seemed confident in me those times, more than I myself. To grow an awkward manner, in days to be a man. I fell short in humbling, now on my knees I kneel or stand.

I'll not be givin' in to the urgin' that comes with my empty stomach. It's been doing its best to get me out of the canister to search for a feast. Still hearin' not a sound of no one, seein' much the less. Thars a wetness in the air that's keeping the damp and coldness alive. A hum, I first thought people get stronger, in some ways louder at times. Mostly, there'll be no finding out whilst I stay in my place. Refuge most assuredly safe, nagging of hunger on the way.

I'll be thinkin' through for a time, then I'll go from wondering to wandering. For shall I grow too weary and can't give myself a hand, this will be where they find me, smothered in piles of happenstance.

With no sense to guess, no windows to breach, am I likely I the deepest or nearest so close? I must be to committing when I've awakened at my post next. Should my hunger not kill me, my thirst and curiosity most assuredly will.

I have awakened by the sound, a collision of two worlds. The sound near as any I've never heard afore. The boat she slowed greatly without a stop. I went into a roll sideways. The slowin' had lain me on my side only to sit us up again with a bang, to something much greater than me. Back and forth we went in most all directions until it felt we must have stopped. I reached out most careful to feel what I might touch. Leaning far, near fallen over, I felt what might be wood. I found, it to be wider hand to hand and higher yet to me.

I waited, long as I would for the next to come, who knew my heart and head in neither had a clue. Should I climb out of my barrel, for till now had served me greatly well.

In a time passin', no way of known how long I came upon a thought. If what has come is to come again or worse, I need see where I'm at.

Without benefit of candle light or brighter no sturdy lantern did I see, I dared to venture outward. Following what might could be a wall. With my hands, so carefully I crept up on my feet, in hopes to feel a ladder, better yet a door.

With no aid in knowing, I felt in touch to left and right. Not sure of being in what is beneath my reach. Is which side the other, a large crate or the boat?

I searched myself for answers, which came slower than the questions. "Oh," said I to me self, "one shall differ temperature in the touch." I decided, I would now put this to use. I gave a touch to either both at one time then themselves. Not an obvious in difference.

"Alright," said I to me self, "how 'bout another way to go?"

I took steps in either way, removed my cap to scratch my itch. It came to me in a landslide, the boat be metal so the crates be made of wood.

Once determining the boat was on my right-hand side, I simply strolled along. In doing this, I tripped and stumbled but did not fall, upon beyond what the eyes could see. After some time, not knowing by any portion of my imagination what awaited in the darkness. There seemed to be some doors or such, no handles could I find. Near there I chanced upon a ladder, that was secured to the wall. I shook with all I had though nothing came of it.

I placed my hands and both my feet on each of a wrung. In a flash of who knows what, it just came to me. Should I need retrace my steps, I'll recall someway, somehow. I will count on each and every step as my hands grasp a wrung. Memory being, not my best suited, I got on my way. At nearly fifty steps an opening showed itself in darkness. Reaching around with all I had, to that which I possessed. There was a landing I must turn and step to right. For a slightest I am open to, nothing more than air. All that holds while I step to the right, one foot and, yes, one hand.

I held tightly for it was a chain and not a rail. I crept along the walk keeping steps in mind. As I reached just forty paces or so the path had all run out. I sought my next alternative, clearly not straight nor down. Of course the ladder did go up. I reversed my last maneuver, going up 'stead of down. Encountering the darkness, though awkward no compare. There were four more up and over's, I finally came up to a door. While something seemed a miss, I continued on.

I've made my way along walkways then up a fixed ladder, repeatedly, so that I could count no further. My legs grew strained and cramped till I could feel no more. The arms I had relied on to count my very steps had felt turned to feel as iron, in attempts by one man's body to emasculate the pain.

Well there, at any rate, I've found a door with knobs plus hinges. My wits find me out of sorts' in anticipation I may seem. A moments more in hesitation, no further shall I be. In my mind decided, open goes the door.

In my view, a party of some chaotic means, complete with fireworks, boats lowered to the sea. Captivated I've become for I can hear the music play. Stepping out and closing eyes so barely can I stand to take it in, as becoming horrified.

I be a lad of simple means, extraordinary be my life though nary midway in my teens. Have not and hoped I never see a dream, as this or lives would be or could be drastically so wronged.

In all splendid naiveté, I find I'm grossly so entrenched in what may be a passing in a restful night's asleep. For my gazed observation has satisfied all I could in wonder. Had I not chose to wander, soon underwater I might been. Pulled down with the vessel seeking a new home. The night is well upon this unsuspecting crowd. The best that I can hope for come the morning hours is to awake on dry land. While now I stand still holding on with what are my aching arms. Was not and in truth not of fear alone I act but with necessity.

For now it has just dawned in me and those around that we are on the rise. The first stack has reached the water; fire's nearly out. Steam has become a bellowing so slightly as her other end begins, slipping and sliding lethargically toward out of sight. The passengers have life vests while the stowaway has none. In the event this is happening and not passing through a dream. Across ageless space in time, the needling of the seam. Where will this leave me, in colors of a rainbow stranded somewhere I've not seen.

In regards to everyone, of course including me, I would like to be remembered, if at all. Be then an assistance to the many as a ship went down at sea.

I started with the children, lost in their own way, having lost a parent maybe two. I countered with the mothers so confused and much distraught, having lost a child or more. To be imagined so I'd lost would cripple all my efforts for the weary to be saved.

I found in my discouraging of men who dressed as woman in their efforts to conceal. What will ultimately limit those that can be saved.

With all the lifeboats filled in partial, the one end she did rise as one stack not quite visible thereafter. Soon would come the break that did shake the world, wrenching the hearts of many as survivors did look on. The splash was great in spectacle. The many of the few they held on for tomorrow, but never would it come.

I then dashed to grab a railing, well known the end was near. I assured myself I'd be awakened far beyond the ocean and its shores.

In all attempts to stay up straight in the cold dark sea, she briefly said goodbye. To all that were and had been loved ones, she bid a fond ado.

A Place Is Called

In strongest revelation that precludes the all, I shall make
further in assuming in presumption heed the call.
Of how I found or came to be upon this
green, soaked reddened field.
Set apart by all I know, this place I'll not call home.
For not, to rest assure I am a fisherman.
In the smallest of the villages, grown to cast the net
I've not awakened unsteady, my toes clinging to the surf.
No, not by what a long shot did as it ripped and torn.
There, is but farmland. As far the eyes could see.
Somewhere in Pennsylvania,
a place called Gettysburg.
I can see the skies in passing, day to night to day.
In the absence set to motion,
I have failed to turn my head, cannot close my eyes.
For days now I have suffered nor, a hunger or for thirst.
I cannot though I dare attempt in
stretching out and of my limbs.
Another day comes yet another night
goes, and here so still I am.
Indignant, I would and could be, if I were not in heaven,
Here among my brethren, both friend and enemy.
Always making room,
For those who pass on by.
All soldiers we'd become.

By Expression We Are Free

In anticipation, we lament.
An accounting, say the we;
"I beg, I plead, I even prayed,"
expectations flabbergast.
"What should be, cannot be this,"
They have made by cause a mockery,
"of my house and homeland."
Answers come, some weeks they don't
I'm sure they will
I doubt, they won't
Shall wonders pass unnoticed
as the stars across the sky.
Think not, all be illustrious,
a marvel of a man,
a chilling as repose,
plowing the same ground.
Again, we sit then stand so wander
over and under again.
The deserved hand all natured,
In peculiar, random signs.
A bee hive giving notice, none,
the honey or the sting.
Clear my mind of what may come,
and that to never see.
If, and when the time comes,
They'll be no certainty.
How or when
Or which the way
See, at times we are so grateful
As we wait and see to be

Story Two

I've wakened from a dream before as different they can be. Still found I in amazement havin' been bestowed. The where, when I find myself, well, has led me to the front stoop of concern.

I spend not much in time, so radiant be the sun. The hours be so measured, as many in a day. I'll be needin' to set it strait once more. Tellin' stories when there's time, so let uncertainty equate to curiosity, for then how many lives?

I see I've there two shoes, one on each my feet, stockings have eluded me once of many times therefore once again. I can tell my pants are drying while underneath still grossly wet. The shirt I bin a wearin' is tangled, torn, and wet. Should anyone but catch a look, a beggar I will be.

The sight of ships with sails travelling up and down the narrows. I see in myself a fondness, more so a curiosity. Breath taking in a world that holds, the majestic deep blue seas. If there were a blind man perched upon this fence, to show none in all regard. The sound, the taste and romance as waves break afore the shore.

Often lost for whys and hows, as like a game to never know, but shall give all effort just to learn. As my clothes begin to dry, I will keep between the muddy road, the sandy beach. So in, I am the challenge add the challenged on a breezy, sunny day. I keep mostly to me self, seem less in pain this way.

Decided on a direction, to what appears a village though closer to a town. Keepin' both eyes and ears handy, in this way I'll learn just what I'm walking to. There's not a lot in schooling, not much to recollect. I make my habits mine, in turn so hope the best. The nearer I get the clearer my eyes become. There is a stream with bridge, a soldier standing watch tween me and most my needs. I grow hungry, not sure in all reality as to when I did eat last. I'll be needin' afore darkness a place to warm my body, lay my head.

In dreams have come and gone there are those meant to arise, diminish with awakenings, to rise and rise again. The wages in the solitude of past the present times. If we are awake in other's minds, are we as a visitor reciting lines? The challenge be recorded amidst, in yours of course in mine. Well then, hell hath no fury greater than a absent minded mime. So stranded yet captive in the movements, when all do subsequently come to motion.

I have what sense the creator gave me. Am waiting off the road a bit, out of the soldier's sight. Made my way clear of the beach, the bridge and town. Behind a clump of trees, I then wait and think of how.

I'll be needin' some clothes and a place to lay, of course not forgettin' something to call a meal. Into town I be in means a way and the path to leave. As my fortune never lets me stranded, there will come what may.

The morning passing, the sun grew high. Praise the saints, here comes my ride. The wagon come there be twin wheels but one horse to pull. Atop the driver's seat there sat a las no younger than I be. On either side a child, one of each I'll say.

I worked to straighten up me self, then stepped out from my shade tree. I gave my best a midday greetin'. My hopes she'd slow down, but no she drove the horses harder. I was lost at such a cost, my stomach remindin' me. I raised one hand, with all my mind to speak. There came a sudden thud I heard, my body strewn upon the road. The hole had not been wide, though deep enough to fall. In placing both my hands to ground, as searching for my wits.

Timely came my look in awkwardness, toward the town in which I saw the wagon to an inching halt. I could nary hear both children urging, her to lend a hand. As she climbed down from her wagon, I bothered not to stand. She began a somewhat solemn stroll, not twelve paces in all. I gently, so carefully lowered to the ground. Had I found answers to my questions, solutions for my needs? Could I stay a bit, a while, or would I be on my way?

She knelt down to assist me, inquired that I be alright. I nodded with a wince, to help the cause in right. We spoke exchanging pleasantries, the wagon waiting in the road. Explained she, having deliveries and a need for some supplies. In suggestion was made, to tell me to stay here behind my shading tree. Evidently not in prosperity, though questions more to ask she said there was time later. With no speech or words to qualify for the wagon she approached, returning with a kerchief full not near enough a meal.

"Before the night arrives," she says, "I'll return to you."

My anticipation alongside my hunger and thirst, were they each to sprout wings would sure to fly. Darkness truly awaits me for I would. Nearest the sun I would glide, if only for the warmth.

I grow weary of not a morsel, fuel for the body I seek. The stranger she was generous, the day now further along. Can you see? I refreshed my thirst from the side of a nearby stream so sparingly. Glancing from 'neath my shelter be a tree; far along down the road, there by the guard on the bridge. Could that be the maiden in kind that passed such a short time ago. I am sure my eyes won't deceive me now, what a rouse to myself would be.

Gently as I ever will, for patiently I can for I must, by the god I love stay at ease for her arrival. Becoming curious of mind and alongside in my thoughts, my hands shake, I can feel. Shall I meet my needs in all at once, will then one at a time. Can I or will I must sleep indoors, nigh beneath the stars tonight.

There is patronage then there is gaggling, a teasing of the sorts I have been and so received. Having reached this point in my existence, I would just casually wipe my nose on my sleeve. My sweet Lord, she is to be a dilly dally with that soldier, in his brightest coat of red.

My broadened sense of sight in witness to the outline of the moon. Noon has reached the past this day, so in myself I embrace immunity. For waiting the stars to see the maid is beyond maiden, am I the damned to sell? I'll not take this for a moment spent in time, not another second for a minute nor by hour. Whom is the focus of my jest in now, as I view upon the amicably there not a soul asides I.

You've caught me off guard. Please assuredly excuse my boast in contents it was. There is still bits and pieces of a performer still inside. You ask of whom I speak of, oh, let me make you see. My youth was of extraordinary elegance, in compare would be none in all. From inside the fortress walls or beyond better said, I wandered where able to each day's end. As through a looking glass into another, my feet as I wondered did send. The further I peered in quiet I went into the garden we met.

Once then out of the home and into the yard, four walls around and a gate. Simply not able to see in or out, one day I'd imagined somewhere to be. To have readily grown into manhood, to return so to pear but once just more. My bag laden with treasure and in so weighted down. There I would be a grown man.

I have fanned your flames of curiosity; I'm not sure I can from your expression either the way is well. I made my move taking a seat so over she had slid, with both children fast asleep so soundly in the back. With no offer to drive made I so none was mentioned nor heard. Into the night four, we did ride.

We were no more an acquaintance by the time we reached the farm. Some the awkward circumstances. Oh look! I see the barn, down the road then up the hill under a full moon's light. Our talk did carry on till off the road we turned, a short ride up the path, there we made our stop. Instinctively, both he and here climbed out through the back.

I helped with the sacks, the rest was for the lad. My newest friend to date knelt in front to start the fire. For the room was rather cold. I encouraged her to allow me. To now, no contribution made by I. Besides, thinkin' to myself then who would make the meal. My stomach was to ask in credit for what I surely could not pay.

The children bid both me and their aunt good night. I had much to learn. I had much to learn in the time I'd be around. Each morning, noon, or night if in my slumber I am found, shake me so, but gently, right down to the ground. If ya wake afore me, you then turn from left to right. Please, think me not the villain. I meant to stay the night.

All is as it seems, though surely never is. You may fool me once, then over and over again. I've the hunger for the obvious and the thirst I dare not quench. What seems not so believable usually is not. If an empty bucket be the truth, then shall an overflowing be the lie. Words can catch and glitter may send you on your way. An action really matters, from the heart you say. If in each day to come closed in the palm of my hand. Could I, would I, should I hold, so tomorrow never comes.

A regret in the making, for in natures nest all comes in its own good time. The more we see, the less we understand.

"I'll see you in the sunrise. Here's a blanket and a pillow. Over there the chairs."

I smiled all but graciously with the waiving of one hand.

"I'll not be sure of who your speaking to, it matters not the same. If you're still here at sunrise we work the fields them morning meal."

I smile, less than halfheartedly, so then I skipped the waive. She slipped behind and closed the door, a good night just the same.

The Joy Is Mine

Out to the highway
Down the road
Back down the trail
Then to the path
Up the hill
Along the river
Next to the stream
I'll go, I can

Beside me, where I go
Whenever, wherever
The height of the wall
The width of the trench
The depth of the hole
Riddle my body
Run down my name

Darts at my picture
Shall cause me no pain
Within the reaches
Out of my grasp
Forewarned and free
No hurry in getting
No reason to run

All is equated
To add up the sums
Past, present, the future
While facing the sun
Both feet in the sand
Like no body's business
She reached out her hand

Onto the highway
Back up the road
Hand in hand
Cross the stream
The trail takes us home
From wherever we come
To where ever we go

My Heaven All Along

A search for new dry land, surrounded by the sea
I waited, then I waited for all the world I'd be
I thought to be a witness of what was washed away
Into the mighty ocean, to the deepest shelf from shore
Far below the skyline, beneath the calming surf
Awaited, plainly I the fool
Limited no more
Was I the sole survivor?
For all eternity
Had I staked a claim?
Had I gone too far?
I dreamt, I wished, I even prayed
Unexpectedly
It was just a parking spot
In a flash of all forbearance
Too late to take back now,
I was a man of my word
I meant nothing by it when I shouted out
Extremely I'd become
To a point was taken all my mumbling
I knew that he had heard me
But I thought he'd sort them out
When I gestured with my mouth
I should not have let it out
I rolled down my window, leaned my head on out
With all the force, I relayed
"You can all just go to hell!"

All went dark, became then white
I opened mine own eyes
I was in a different place
Though very much the same
I'd sent them all to purgatory
On their way to hell
I searched for the conclusion
It came, not easily
Like a coin tossed in the fountain
To heaven have been tossed
Not so different is this place
There bears familiarity
I've been in heaven all along

Every Day Is Sunday

He wandered into town, one bright, so sunny day
At first, there was amusement
Walked he both sides the street
A wider stride for only those
For whom would keep the pace
Taken twice as many steps
Of those in lost the race

First, says I, too he in jest
I simply, saw none other way
He smirked, then leaned to speak
And spoke, he had
Assuredly
Known no other way, I'd venture

He said to me, as I to you
What is your point despair?
With one finger in one ear
A sign to please repeat
Once more
Not twice or three nor four

Handing me, the golden plate
A chance for all that cared
A coin tossed in the fountain
I stopped and gave it all I had
Quite naturally
A point was soon complete

Inquiring he must
In rhetoric
From one breath to the next
All had been assumed
Resurrected
For the next

In utter contemplation
I sat down in the pew
At first my hands were folded
Placed right in front of me
A shortened red colored pencil
A form I could now see

I skipped all that mattered not
My first, last name, and such
The block was small, denying
Me, a given chance
I placed my word in single
By an arrow, it said over

I figured, all in all
Must be, what's meant to be
As I'm sitting on this park bench
My handheld phone in hand
Observing all I can
Dismissing what I must

All came to me so simply
Much, later on in life
I've partied with the haves
Celebrated the have nots
Looking for examples, each
The dos and the do-wrongs

From the pulpit came;
In reading of the words
A reading not familiar
Though likely, I had heard
A rock to skim the surface
Formed ripples by the stone
Across the, once great pond

A slice and dice to words

The greatest in outpouring
I reached into the plate
Dropped my note, then left my future
In the solitary wake
My offering came, in what I'd said and done
In addition to my note

I deposited a nickel
Took a quarter back

Story Three

I am found in thought this morning, the appearance of the day. In breathing be the challenge in the struggle of each gasp, I take. There feels a substance in a thickness to the air, never did I find. A grit to spread by movement of the slightest touch. I'll not witness earthly shadows for the absence of the sun, not a clouds accumulation, none other than much dust in volumes I have never yet to see.

The evening's darkness as assuredly it comes, will come by a snap of fingers. For there be not so great a change, there be one just the same.

In avoidance of the field work, a missing of a meal. I seem in a formed stability of a worn out type of house. I'm a rambling sort this journey, from one to the very next. Dastardly I am, not to dwell on what simplicity can't or won't explain. If all viewed is conjecture how limited are I?

Dressed not for the season by the weather I'll abide. Where there are in gentler times so grand in passing with the ages, in good to be a man. Now in fact I see so aided by the times, my hat, my shirt and shoes have each seen better days. The stockings in need of mending, in each shoe is no surprise.

I dare, for I know I must gape down into this dirty glass. My greatest concerns arise of who came before me to where they placed their mouths. What a world we live in, if only passing through.

At next the door swings open as were the winds possessed in hell. A shorter wait preferred for the air to clear, by then I see the face of which has grown an age austere. Her questions fired rapidly, none in answers I prepared. Yes, I then repeated yes, I'm searching for a sustenance for which I am prepared to work. Follow me she gargled, with a sound of lost and straggling teeth.

While in not a practice to acquiesce the superlative forged judgment not I n kind. In my own; the abrupt fashion in that I pass on past the door, in closing, nearly knocked me to the floor. All became then equal as I watched the maiden stroll, one leg being shorter for the all in all. My sympathy I straddled for in my own humility, the parts they all did come though some came not to work.

Life, be so much more than a tragedy, room so there to laugh. Much has tried to limit my time now here with you. In obvious so kind most and all have failed.

When the storms come rowdy, the spray into the sails, I give my all in recitation while clung tightly to a rail.

For now! Yes, for now, I am where few do care to venture, in less to meet a dare. I ride all in circumstance as a man with no tradition as no goals yet to achieve.

Breakfast came so quite well, the mug and bowl and, yes, the spoon were such to behold. The meal itself found me in great need, may tomorrow never come.

Down the road I followed so to gather all. I been informed there'll be a pick and shovel, of which I'll have a need. Others, there are acquired out of each week's pay.

A week here I have worked and spent; so hardly paid the room and board, if among the all the grandest were totaled in the world, could not this make the list. A thousand pardons in regret, much too far ahead I get when anxious. Horrified and lonely each time the whistle blew, was I on my way or had a cave in doomed my neighbors?

Today it was the pay day, left over not so much. Enough to have a drink with the lads, in those I am to know the best. Not to frolic or be tardy for the evening's meal. There may be gaps a-tween a teeth or two, a wobble in the walk, insult atop injury most every time she talks. Now I've listed attributes that I seem to know the best. If truth be told and hear for here it must. The best kept jokingly a secret she does have, is both a catching wink followed by a seductive smile. Serious on occasion in jesting now I'm not. For I've become a time or two a victim, when in my direction she does both at once. Individually not so much.

There have been a few in number occasions I did excuse myself, quickly but so carefully from the table flew. In following her in all good speed to the back yard we did go. We had in previous, went just up the stairs. I found her at an open door, my manhood stood in check. She winked and smiled then snorted. "There be seats for two."

I was and had been needin', with my trousers down and underwear, I took my nightly post meal seat. In talk we both went on for a bit till we both were done. Then we went the back stairs, right up to her room. Some things we done and some we didn't. I think she understood. Though her heart was in it, she claimed there'd be a bill. Off to bed I went, in hopes to dream the night away. Thoughts came in greater bundles than nights afore this one.

He who might I be if I am not, in who or what I say. Shall I be a subjugated hero in turned a villain's eyes? Will I or will I not, walk where robbers tread? I'll desire not a realm, no palace, in swordplay find me dead for no ambition found me here. To seek the prime existence with a meal served proper time. A glaring of preponderance in stealing eye to eye. From ear to ear a throat is sliced, by there be no such command. To rule one shall resuscitate that peace with loving hands.

The taller man makes no greater marks, than he whom holds half strength. May so both be remembered when they live and forgotten when each not. In the eternal eventuality, not known till the fare is paid. Hopes, the dreams like mustard seed will spread across the bread.

All the doldrums seem necessity, in truth not real or seen. I'll not fear or loath to worry for in my palms be air. Every day in each, I awaken as a dream, not forged in curiosity, nor one paddle handy on the stream.

Like the brook will trickle, accompanied my mind, let it drip so gently to my fingertips, when I portray a dragon extended wings and breathing fire, shall be what I say, no difference and no recourse nigh remand.

Yours or Mine

Furthermore the wind cries, sharply from the south
Tears they will thus scatter all the way northeast
Sneezing out to sea
While coughing fits in gusts
come out of the sky
searching for a hanker chief
somewhere, to wipe its eyes
Of maybe yours or mine
Of timing, it shall tell
Spinning like a top
across the prairie's edge and center
seemingly particular
of what does go and stays
Marking the conversion
of rubble from most homes
Store fronts boarded up
many have been strewn
This message has been brought to you
not for you alone
Nor for you and me

Story Four

So through the corridors in no repetition thus infrequent have I seen, to stand face to face in where and when I've been. To cross the path of those I've known in another place and time, may need to lead me to a backwards motion. in course there be no need. At times, I chose relax to that of the sharp ax. Not bonded as a servant or stretch upon the rack. While each day's eyes to open far less a penny or a pound. My permanent street and number prevent and cause confusion for receiving any mail.

When I pass on by, no need to waive or shout, what comes between the king and queen by the poet has been saved. A wink and smile says it all. Good day, kind sir, you'll have in letting go the all.

Traced by Time

The seams are wide, way down in side
Where to forage for the real
Empirical, spells disaster
If one, stands in one's own way
Thrust upon the singled pole
Hear, the mighty roar
Standing straight at hell's own gate
A situation poor
The shield, though casts no armor
A sword carved from the tree
Hath loosened what came swift
Rage in torrent spoke the night
Streams like rivers came to filled
Awake the dragon, twice one night
The bridge, had thus been crossed
Was, to a mighty feat or hexed
Rumbling, of the earth
The lion raged, the deal was caged
Somewhere, tween here and there

Story Five

In all of we take in, are we more than obligated to send out? To the originator and those that stand about, word for word as blow for blow. In we all divine, do we then condemn ourselves?

As often as I wake and so, but just one more time, I am not always sleeping more a daydream in my mind. For and only for when I have awakened, will the present become yesterday as well the future to the past. If I were because I am today, a riverboat captain steaming full ahead. Loathing for the flatboats and the barges that drift into the way. My immediate response is needed so not to drive these onto the banks or worse.

I covered the night watch to just about sunrise, a member of my crew was ailing. I bid my relief good day and I was on my way. My cabin lacking inspiration at a glance becomes in awe though I am a handy man. There be no fancy curtains or in color draperies. I made my round of all the decks while expressing pleasantries. Into the gaming room I trudged into clear the air. Often in the all night longs hostilities arise. There been some talk, combatants in the air disguised as best they can. A lot of collars getting hotter in congress these here days.

May come a ruckus maybe not, we'll have to wait and see. I will keep my crew and boat both ready for when whatever may it come. Up and down the river, a bit to left or right. Let cause and effect in both be money, let the devil make his deal. If one be in the going, so shall be received.

To place a wage on one outcome seemed a certainty, the devil resides within us all in bewildering fain attempts. In capturing the moment, for a lifetime will to beg. To earn, to spend, to do again, marauders of the stage from where we all had come in playing of the game.

I'll a needle to my eye, should all seem to pretend. I strive to drive this steam propelled in and out my days. In all my love will miss her, in a wealth sincerity, for to anticipate another, another rainy day.

I won't sit at the table, nor will I deal the cards. Not now to read the faces, in no way know to raise or fold. If the jester wears a thorny crown, why would we chose to differ? Would the winnings then be traded for all hypocrisy? Is a loss a loss, if at the table I sit naked and so very cold. Shall the world around be enclosed so not to breathe. Will the warmth exceed the stranger's ingratuity. Are most so to be taken by the smile on their face, the other will exhaust a heart worn on the sleeve.

Will listen to the paddles being driven by the steam, I am at a disadvantage as lay me down to sleep.

Awake me in the prairie, fresh with the morning's dew. Let the cattle graze, let the wind come to its rest. The stars will spread so vastly, wide beyond my eyes. I am certain not, if I do to seek, for nothing is my all. Believe me not in closing, goodnight one and all.

Stowed away below, 'neath the cargo hold, be there all so many to accompany the few. In piloting this vessel in and out of tides and storms. I shall ever ach so deep of my responsibility. I ask no man, a woman, child to do in a day's work by lash.

Freedom so by nature in not an attribute; an award, no, it is a right. Ignore not the principle, to look another way. I'll ask no one to live as I would not a second to the day. Here I sit in transport; natures absurdity, hence forth through the ages, man simply crushing man. The meek not be the eaten for the chosen few, agreed to nothing more in substance the mortar held, not true.

In a mind we search and dig for answers, in hope to explain away the traditions that may come our way. What if then the future, have then lost along the way.

I close my eyes, upon my bed I sit. Will I simply visualize; first there is no furniture, then gone the floor and walls, the wind carries the roof away, so on with the shudders and a door. Tighter are my eyes as gone the house and barn, there the village next. No country, land, and world.

To squeeze my eyes much further, in sure my head will pop as parts shall drift in air. There, gone, the sun, the moon, and stars, only me just waiting by. To imagine the beginning, with all smarts I muster yes intelligently.

A smattering of wonder, the humming in my ears alongside the sun its rays with particles is eking its way through. Morning has arrived; awaken I must too.

The peek I take in habit formed along the way to seeing only what awaits. Nothing yet familiar. Praise God to grant me the day, allow me but a smidgeon, and I will be on my way. In time I will awaken and greet the world good day.

To Remove My Cap

Son, how there would they find you
On this wondrous, illustrious day

As goes on the travel, about the hills and ways
Not of near your home or haven

Into foreign lands the search
Has taken those allotted, torn

That deem you not as lost
In a moment's still entirety

As locked between dreams, reality
The date will continue marching, as it must now

Will fear not of redoing steps in perpetuity
A journey gladly embarked upon, once more

Altogether favorably again, again
You have and always will

Be a whisper in the ears
For all who went to serve

Not able to return
More than just a memory

A time for a silent moment
To remove my cap

Father in Heaven, thank you
For those who may or may not find, thank
you for continued mending of
the shattered, broken hearts of those who gave it all.
Everything they had, above and so much more.
Down through the infant's history
From one war, engagement, conflict
To one mission then the next
Those who keep and kept our liberty
Closest to their hearts

Amen

Story Six

Up! Now up I tell you! There are bills to be paid to the likes the butcher and the landlord. I will not be late another day because of you. You delay till the latest in moments in hope all will show clear. I pulled on and up my pants, fastened the rest, leaped into my best shoes. In need of a shine they are. My two friends will be here soon in hopes of not needing to gather me up.

I've nary a second truly, I'll check myself in the mirror as a friendly reminder to me. I give myself a smile, ready on my way. I risk further dispute with me self, with that came a knock at the door. I said out loud with all my calm, "Come in. I'm ready to go."

The door with its noisy old hinges opens as I put on my smile. In through the door's way she sashays into my humble abode. Quite obvious he at a bow with the straightest of knees back out the loudest of doors. Down the rickety steps, as both safely held to the rail. No broken bones needed this early, all poor joking aside I entail.

Into the most lavish of carriage, into the door I did climb. Next, came the most deserving in soul she has in her steps alone, being the gentleman I. In all my restraint I resisted to help while being coy to the sky. To appear as best I could not captured by her bust.

My time been better, most known as not. While her comes a man not to meet; The owner the shop I live atop, also collects rent from me. He chanced a glance as we rolled by, so infinitely my lateness to pay. Give or take another day or on my way I'll be. With all courage and understanding, she whispers across to me, "Do you believe there's time for breakfast?" In this she held the key, I'd not check my pockets in eventuality. Like a dog I beg almost every morning. Be it so nor be it not, for the time being will not go hungry but living in the street. All irony to set aside fate has crept my way.

A good meal had by we as if there were but three, now off to work we must. Employed by a daughter's father shelters some circumstance. Most are fun in dawning till by his door I pass. Truth be told, for I must, who would hear my lie. I am not to pretend, so I collect a salary for nothing which I do. Now, and truly now I am standing in fate's way.

That took very short in time for it seemed so well rehearsed. By the time that noon arrived I had been well packed. Jobless, soon to be without a home. I shall share the fortunes of the street, now there is where I've gone.

Most of my belongings were but a cluttered mess, shoved packed do tightly in drawers that were once my desk. Out the door in front, right away I made a left turn into the empty alley way, waiting there they were. I found an empty barrel, my belongings shall call home. From my vantage point I caught a glimpse, about halfway down the alley there was the carriage stopped. If he and she be truly friends let the moments in torture begin. They are but a couple, to both I be a friend.

In my most uninspiring moment, the act of nothing wrong. I played it to the hilt, I did not know they'd play along. Up beside me pulled the coach and stopped in such a random choice. The he addressed me as "good man," So let the games begin. Sir, my good man, could or would you better to recommend an eatery in far above your means? I felt my hands to clenching as she hid her face from me, fortunate for all the game did not ensue.

Invited I became, for start a meal would do. They each went on for quite some time with pity and such woes. I looked up on occasion just to take a breath. If this was all I was to eat for the coming days, I was compelled to make it count.

Into what possessed a quest for an experienced finality in wrenching of my heart and soul. I pondered the immediate resolution of that which places my back against the wall and my ego thusly to the corner. I will survive and outlive my usefulness to a large and impartial plateau. When my means exceed this described, I will as I say, venture onward thus upward as to prevail.

I detect a misapplied reasoning of my logic. I am with pockets filled to bulge and overflow a wealth of knowledge as I view. I shall for I can portray me to myself, therefore assuredly a commendable audience in any venue, my desire.

In need not closing my eyes, as I see the characters in the light of day. In this the lines will practice then so savor by rehearsing. For the noon previews the night, in turn bring the footlights to the stage.

This meal shall stretch to cultivate thus captivate my waistline. In need I am shall be, while seemingly much destitute then the cure shall be, predictably a lie.

Will, for always has been, the sympathies are played to a packed house. Those who are upon those who won't, see by candle's light. Wilt they once from the vine to nary shed a tear, for the empathy will spread itself with such the largest spoon. By night's end a dawning for the matter of a gratitude, maybe scorned again.

To my quest my cavalry in need I shall return, in closing of my eyes. For golden slumber's reaching deeply not shall rehearse me not this way. I find my ego in discomfort, its back supports the wall.

May I awaken fit and cheery recovered of it all. Onto another journey, admission is the price to what the guide may ask intuitively each day.

Tears in Her Eyes

There is quiet in her silence
I offer spare change for her thoughts
Then she grins and shakes her head
Says something I've forgotten
Walks into the other room
She stops to dab her eyes
Something I did reminded her
Of the past, I guess
Simply put I've failed her
In what I did or did not do
Along with what I did not know
Time has passed and years gone buy
There is quiet in her silence
Things have come and gone undone
Stretched out what is and isn't
Who could ask for more

Story Seven

In stroking for my own and all its encounter this day, I strive. Not likely the best in, or will ever I. My hat I wear as humbling satisfies the coat and rack. I have awakened with my eyes still, yet tight.

The at first a murmur, somewhere off into my left. There and then continues on closer to my right. Be there no recovery, have exposed myself to all. I anticipate, to a dozen maybe more. Sidebar conversations a minor distraction, of which not prepared for.

For responses to the questions I have yet to recollect, will be a conglomeration. Indeed I need but just a glance of an agenda. Something to get me safely off the railroad track. Fear not and I won't for all is much I see. A day as any other, a deal or a decision of that I yet must remove unvanquished by my own hand.

I'll side with one, agree with most then occupy my seat. It's got me this far so far, now to open eyes. Figuring, I've showed my hand so early in the day so long in length. I am struggling with a likelihood, that is, something is amiss. Has caused at times a strain, so often times as this.

There times when I have slowed to just a creeping, for how far I have crept I have arrived no speed at all. Then I am asleep, still hear around me the verbal all in all.

Shall dreams be what I seek, I've found them in a pyre to the sky. Where this is some interest for me, my thoughts do slip and slide. In a manner all accustomed I only see what is there.

An ability to misinterpret; Your thoughts mixed in mine, will result to cause some if not all, in mass confusion. The audience, be two or more to fall, a victim to my unintended prey. One shall be mindful for what they beg and plead. In the eventuality all does come the way. I'd rather be on dry land than I, one boat, one paddle, going round and round. All that comes as darkness is not all in nightfall found.

In my boat I'll curl up and lay myself and my head down. Awkward may it be, by the time that I am found. I'll dream upon dreams of that at which has and has not come to pass. Still, yet I know difference. In a reading I can tell.

Stretched out in the boats floor with my arms spread wide and length, in my way I greet the early morning sun.

With the dusks arrival came a greeting tide. Waves had found to grow in turn the rocking of my boat. As the darker night became, I could see plainly I was not still nor alone. We, me and the boat had acquired passengers. A humbling style of dress each wore. Alongside what appeared to be nets for catching fish.

Was not my concern alone also, the bearded ones had risen, to wake the one alone. Calmly, without the slightest concern or worry he stood unaided in the surest of footing, with aiming of look at each as shaking his head side to side. Something said he in a language I did not know at the time, in addition my ears had grown weary. In a few, the shortest in moments the wind and sea did subside not yet in total agreement, by the likes of you and I. All was calm in seemed right; he laid down once more.

The remaining ones did mumble well beyond under their breath, in varied levels they exceeded of this for a language not I known. In not so much the language as strange to me the spirit of. Had their leader not saved in his efforts us, of one in all.

There came a need in slumber I, so in the rest I take. My comfort in the hands of one young, bearded man.

There be a power in known reality so to speak and see; however there be greater in the splendor of thy dreams.

The Yearning

Where there is hunger be there yearning
of each love and peace
Set aside what differences
for in the path each wait
Upon the reach and thought
of all will to surmise
The catalyst be stored
so, in a hollow core
Stretch to reach
Up on each shelf
higher gets the climb
Until tops the mountain
A valley be of far and wide
as earthly may be seen
names into the ledges
of we who came to be
The dawning of the age so
rocks along with arrows
can simplify the matter
where the straights are narrowed
For there is hunger, as yearning cast aside
of each the Love has garnished little Peace
embellished on what differences
make and break to ache

Story Eight

I am myself in darkness, awakened I believe, by courtesy a thunderstorm, a boom. Sure I am as I can be, must been a gun. A wait before I return to sleep. This time comes a bang preceded by a shriek. Proceeded by a contact with the wall, a grunt imposes quite suddenly followed by a fall. Possibly, may accurately describe the contact of the flesh in number there be two.

The moon is up the sun not, so night time must still be. A yelling and a brawl go on uninterrupted mostly through might, awaiting morning hours. All repeated in so many an event as if coming through the wall, itself. Makes me think to wonder, will one or both survive. To whom, will greet the constable when he does arrive?

From my rented room, I hear a knocking at a door. Now that all was quiet no need of saving anyone, though obviously a need to wake the dead. On urging of all others, in hope to save a life. For all the while waited on the constable, for all the neighbors knew was a human sacrifice. A little less war and a little more peace, sounds of a Christmas Card. I think to myself as peacekeepers drive on down the road. What causes men to do this, cannot they see how wrong it is? Sons see what they are able, learn what they feel they must. If daddy eats standing on his head, then so why don't I.

Am I getting what I pay for, in the middle of the night? In all sincerity walking through the hall I hear a panting noise up against a door, scratching wood with sharpest nails. A thud and then a bang, is something being pulled across the floor? Mine peeked in curiosity, until I came upon the morning's air. Now, been awake to travel to a job somewhere. In all hopes I'll find there is less drama, within a worlds despair.

I've tossed and turned so turned and tossed the entire night away, asleep on the couch. Some wild dreams I've had, with the bizarre dream I shall have. Some are fascinating, while others just are not. My soul aches in dreams of horror, my back from a couch.

Story Nine

I was of want and need to become a carrier of the daily news. Packed tightly, overloaded in worn out canvass bags, supported by a strap. While the strain and wear to my shoulder diminished as the route proceeded by my efforts each day. Those I had observed trudging up back driveways, often wagons, shopping carts on the heaviest of days. Stick ball played against a square home plate painted on the tavern wall, touch football in the vacant lot and hockey for the coldest days.

Much has changed to find me living largely in the alleyways; dark corners called my home. I am patronized by some, excluded by most, ultimately defeated by none. In search of part time work a couple hours a day.

In the crevasses of fortunes spent, my life's been lived. I'll return to in a whim while traversing gold and silver; adventures are for travelers, in ambition using time, while I simply harbor maximums in the journey's vessel, a repair in time. My awakening are many, trials and tribulation few. I come here to ease my outlook as well for my mind. If the windmill be a dragon I'll have diamond clusters for each eye. In which the logic goes, the queen of clubs is not the ace of spades.

In my hand I am making notes to hide inside my drawer. I'll keep them a secret, until the stories told. A collected work in history, not in me prepared. The note's I'll make May and June to register for telling of such tales.

For now, returning to my quarters in the shadows. Well-arranged between a garage and a shed. All is not forever then shall never seen. Excuse me while I greet my guest, the likes of never been. It's time we bedded down.

In this barn of luxury, I spend most a day. Not far below the line, goes the likes of you and me. Upward with the rising sun, well past the sun goes down. There good to us in most respects, a roof a floor, four walls. Including meals if all behave.

Most the family has grown and gone, except the youngest daughter. She is cute and round, parading with her dolly in and out the gate. She has grown in slight referring to us as, Mother and Father's hired hands. It is unquestionably a tremendous assumption to think that we are paid. We often find to laugh that the young one thinks that we can come and go. The innocence perturbing, the naiveté abundantly enough to spread around. We may sing in the sunshine, as we work the fields. Not without thoughts, considerations of who we merely are.

As darkness is upon us, work is all complete. Nearing toward my shelter, asleep I need to be. For all encompassing in nature, for all that has come to pass, that faith will move the mountain. As my head to pillow, so in will be my prayers.

The Wall of Mine

Behind the wall I imagine
Created there to be
Another world existing in entirety
Grown from subtle measures
At least it was before
All the rage of fear and loathing
Like as never seen implored
Stone my body, free my soul
First throw don't hesitate
If better felt a reason
Make it no mistake
If so that endures you
Brings nature to its knees
Atop the wall I see I do
The mystery at hand
Graven images withstanding
All known solidified
Higher even yet, standing on my toes
The utter playground waiting in all its infancy
Now it's time, I've got to go
The plow truck has arrived
Off the wall I've leapt
My day is in your hands

Story Ten

On the edge the bed I sit, I wipe my crusty eyes. The day has come to greet me, to the window I will rise. A school bus for the neighbors, I am to wait for one more year. I am decidedly the oldest, I have made up my mind. There is a baby brother, he gets in my way. He throws my blocks then cries, when he gets pushed away. I am small so many things, by patience I a short. He barely walks and never talks, what am I to do?

I have to wait for everything, just to go outside and play. I don't know what the big deal is I'm almost turning three.

Dinner takes forever, Father works most nights, and I have to share my bath. Bedtime is such a hurry; one day I will figure it all out. I have to read myself a story, I know most the words. I am getting tired …

The Tournament

From the East our day begins
To the West our day does end
In the Morn our Sun does rise
By noon high in the sky
During, while our evening
The Sun and Moon pass by
Bye hours early morning
They once again reply
To the call of Nature
Creativity, sublime
If the Sun, Moon and planets
For which the stars align
Bear, peaceful coexistence
I must, ask this question
Why but Why but Why
In cordial circumstance
Put all differences aside
Let the Leaders argue, in the ring and out
Make a tournament it all
The winner's purse may count
Construed as what is small
But the prize be golden
Each leaf all trees be green
Of all the lives be spared
Let the monuments to anger
Stay great, in disrepair

Story Eleven

By one mentioned or another, I have since become retired. Where hunger exceeded thirst has worked out from beneath. In all I'll not declare endurance over time as great.

    I awoke a morning yesterday to hear the doctor say, you have a touch of this and always have and will, all of your given days. In nodding of the absolute, I had at times thought why I was portrayed this way. Moments, in thought most friendly were nearly, mostly that. The teasing of a friend and how he made his walk.

    Leaning ever forward like a fall was in the works, the right swinging every way, the fingers tied in knots. At time attempts to balance as reaching for a breeze. Awake I've been since yesterday, sometime after morn. I have not been scarred in detail, eventually no harm. If this be the deal as real and not just in a dream. I will arise for the occasion to play hand I'm dealt.

    For now I have grown tired, lay down my weary head. All is not consuming, let final ever come. Let my soul soar like an eagle to illuminate the moon. For passage see the gypsy with her crystal ball.

The Likelihood of Woman, Man

How would you describe
Compared to, what you cannot see
Would you paint a picture, a work of art to be?
Shall it be discovered, in words that just won't hide?
Could it be a magic trick, a slighting of the hand
A daring feat of enchantment
Possessed along the way
By what you cannot know, not seen
Will you shout it from the roof tops
Shall you paint it on the walls
Along the bridge, the overpass
The base of buildings tall
On trucks that stopped along the way
Can you hide it in the garage, locked inside four walls
If the lock won't lock, how would you keep in?
In the likelihood of Woman, Man
It could not be a secret until the count of ten
Thoughts can bend and twist,
while the crowd throws stones once more
So you tear my skin and you break my bones
There'll still be no distracting, from the blowing wind
Though I cannot see it
I know where it comes from

Story Twelve

My footprints toward adulthood have been covered by the snow, washed away by rain. I see the colored imagery in both rainbows and run offs. One day as good the next in leaving a youth wasted, far behind. It attracts me as a magnet, leaves emaciated grindings in the flask. For what experience has given, leave disaster in the past.

If not my love of summer I'd find myself behavin', I no doubt would be staying here at home. No I went to a party, what could happen did. The earliest in morning, the next day stirring me, In the highest hopes it had all been but a dream.

It came upon me slowly though come to me it did. At a party for preseason, the game on the TV. The keg was getting warmer outside under roof. Still no doubt from the sun. In need of more ice I agreed to run.

I grabbed a lad with surer hands, a stronger back than I. His dismay was recognized as obvious. I assured "we won't be long." We procured four tall bags of ice, we were on our way.

Then we hurried down the length of road and stopped, 'cause I was really sure. Opened up the trunk a bag for each our hands. Rushing toward the house, in a hurry through door. Into the kitchen, not sure where all have gone.

In the sink the ice went, I followed in the living room. Someone had changed the channel. I changed it and sat myself back down. I noticed in the corner, was curled up in the couch. A man, a woman, two small children about to die of fright.

I glanced at my companion, he motioned toward the door. I agreed not saying anything, no stammering nor words. To the car we flew, in lieu of an apology. Something had escaped me, we had forgot the ice. A minor fly in the ointment at this so awkward of times.

My passenger was visibly annoyed. His plans so greatly upset, was soon to change his mind. As we pulled up to the house and parked, something was not right. I pulled myself together and followed on inside. We were for all intention now at the right house. To the front door we went slowly, with a quiet knock. Both doors in and out were closed.

One friendly neighbor down the block two doors and across the street, beckoned with a waive. I amused her with my presence as she started to explain. Moments after leaving the first police car came. Just a minute later came the second car, unmarked. They arrested some, those that did not get out in time, they were placed in handcuffs and hauled away. The keg was confiscated.

I pulled away and wondered, what else may go wrong? A Summer thus a summer, be it three months long. A nap I took when I got home, a meal precluded this. Sometime after dark, though early in the night, I had another dream. As it came to be the one just told about, was real.

The Frame

He'll not be obligated to ways you will dispel
What passes for the anger
the fear you hide all well
Standing in the looking glass
A glance prescribed each day
what appears in a reflection
will mark the table set
A room among its furnishings
Curtains hung so right
Enlightened be the candle
its struggle to stay bright
All be of the flourishing
Awakened by the evening
becomes the such contrite
a hold unto, much excelled
The count will not elude
what in you, past denied
In among the fury
The rampant cries of strife
Beyond the soliloquy
of ringing is still his
For awkward stands in circumstance
Where happenstance as may
the illusion strokes the brush
A canvas as is wide

Landscapes and bouquets
hidden my a mountain
snow covered by the rain
awaiting that which thunders
in thoughts to wash away
Richly be no value
when purse is bursting for relief
The Sun, the Moon and Stars
Of painting
have fallen down
behind the frame

Story Thirteen

The root of cleaver thought, the stories go along. Some become quite masterfully adored, others hang so carefully yet barely on the wall. Life is made of selections, choices, challenges waiting for the bell to ring.

In, let there be such new such new in days to occupy the clock. At dawn shall come, the night may go, shall surely come again. So, in to reach for all as never will again.

To covet all the air in less to breathe once more. Hold a deed in a clenched fist till is not a mend. In, hold yet one dearer, then the other beat as still. The drum sounds as the heart doth, in counting down the hour of a day.

Allow thoughts so they enter, for a meaning and a touch. Hold to cease the lively in one's length a measurement, yet from beneath the scope.

In, let there be such few in days to occupy the mind. At dawn shall come a new sunrise, though the setting in the west. All that comes and goes, shall surely come again.

I'll awaken to the verses, for in times again, not heard in voice nor form. There be none assured in imagery or a parting cloud, however come they do so they must. A myriad of terms.

A though comes an idea, I nod with a smile.
The next line comes no hesitance, I sit up in bed.
Afore the third completed, I am on the stairs.
In my faith, a memory deserves.
Sometimes, seems the stars collide.
In believing in and of the all, have covered yet the most.
Unveiled in not a mystery, gone from the masses hid.
Found again in centuries, in sleep among the dead.

I'll close my eyes, in not my mind.
The glory found anointed, bares its truth in fruit.
Art need not be freedom, yet freedom be the art.
I find myself, this journey not in omission,
of what I've sought and found.
Perched high, beyond the steps,
reflecting near a pool.
We possess, the spot where we are found.

Days of now gone memories I have captured in so dreams. I will applaud the author who with his words described of, all a nation in things we shall not hide. There is love, some kindness found, in whose name was as Abraham.

I return to slumber, if so be this the dream. There will be the awakening, sometime may today.

The Daily News

Are *we* merely caretakers?
Keepers of a faith
Watching of the animals
Grouping the unruly, into tiny squares
Ambiguous at times
Spelled out expectations,
All around the world
Most spectators are
Crossing over borders, each and every hour
Back and forth the tides shift
As they truly will
Washing out to sea
Such a thunderous in noise
Are *we* then, the caretakers?
Caring for the land?
Drilling down for oil every chance we get
If not then, as expected,
able at a stretch
Are we then our brother's keeper
or just our sister's overlord?
How-about our-selves,
treated like used cars
Wearing of a body, standing in the rain

Drug around as helpless
Inflict, avoiding pain
Are *we* merely caretakers?
Failing at the forum
The plat-form stays the same
What, should set us free
Give us love and hope
Away—superiority
Namaste

Story Fourteen

A burning desire stops no man
Unless he snuffs out his own flame
The lighting and shadows
A candle, a lantern
An absence in both, a good wick
Sustaining a fire, burning inside
Retain the sewn, in desire
A wanting of all that is known
Mediocrity being the prize
A dull ache as the true winnings
Abysmally mistaken
Flow not, tears from the eyes
There, belittle remarked in a measure
They have had the haves and have not
The play of a word, in roll of a dice
In a moment, shall pigs not fly
I'll not match wits for ware
For in good conscience will not
In the end, to all envy
I live here among the most gracious
Naked upon all the rocks

The Bark Is the Bite

He—a raider, the shaper, a molder of words.
Thus, be the character a leader for all?
Enthralled by what works, as seldom, so heard.
A quote from the last page, accordingly
yes, appropriate nah.
Daring for most, would, you think so?
For the dimming of lights.
One herder of cattle, crashing it seems,
Right down the main street,
Through dawn's early light.
The he, be the puzzler;
A tone he'll bequeath, to none other than,
The sound of his own, empirical in choice.
Derivatives flowing, by way of his voice.
A call to the wild, observantly so.
The meek, then the melting,
Shall return home.
By choice not desire,
Then all are to guess as well if they had.
Exodus, by nature will eventually come,
to port in surviving,
For they know, they shan't hide.

Story Fifteen

I have come to my thoughts under a bridge, in truck buried in snow on a road quite traveled by us. The truck I am in, its engine has ceased to spin, so pulled over have become me. I believe the crank case is dry.

A lovely day I thought to myself, all the sights one coating to see. I stood in the road with my thumb in the air, my lack of good fortune to see.

A truck came yes barreling faster than he, was going to see me, so out of the way I dove. The winds of change though pushing snow hard came about my way. One careful and experienced driver was traveling at what we'll call a safe speed. I saw the passenger side with window down, she asked if I needed a ride.

I smiled first, then thought again of what I was going to say. In the utmost of gratitude in stating that she was so kind. The pleasantries were piled on until I could no more. She followed with a "Please get in then we'll talk some more."

There was a passenger in front of me, seated in the front passenger side. He was headed to the airport, in so I wished him well. We chatted three, four minutes until my exit came. I still had quite a walk, in truth awaiting me. By now I was not able to see in front of me, my hands or frozen feet. My feet kept moving, forward I leaned until in the door I fell. I stayed close to the floor, until the alls did melt or thaw.

In summary: Some days it rains, some days it snows, most days it all works out. Up to and including, asleep and soaking wet stretched out on the floor. The distance one may travel in a hurricane, a blizzard or a flood. These all add up to nothing if you never make it home.

Tangled Gratitude

From his boat at sea, the fisherman saw
His net had become tangled
In not being alarmed
For in the boat, was only he
What seemed, so thought to be
A large fish in his net
In all reality a swimmer
Giving what he had
to get to where he'd gotten
Into the boat the swimmer climbed, unaided
He caught his breath shook off the rest
Continued on evasive
The fisherman waited patiently
for gratitude, never will to come
The swimmer leaped out from the boat
To where, he had just come
Exhaustion reached the fisherman
in which frustration was brought on
So exclaimed was the rescuer, nearing tears to hide
I pulled you from my nets
in hope to save your life
Now you have returned to where you came
My good fellow in all earnest
grateful I would be
if all, in what you saw
was that, so easily to see
I am out here for a swim as natural could be
Your boat was in my route
In accordance with my efforts
You drifted into me

Story Sixteen

Where near the highways cross is where I sometimes breathe the air in freedom. No, not an ounce of charity will I need receive. When I am found, in cause to relocate my joyous times survive. Free of all responsibilities, a debt to no one owed. I am dreaming or believing, a matter and it not. Beyond myself not influenced by a martyr or a rock. The cave ins come momentous, as in a cloud of dust. Rain itself shall wash away if blood comes from a stone. To have no virtue then absent sin on a scale of ninety-nine. Solutions, absolutions all waiting in a line. Who went last, then who's next the circle does entwine.

My shelter holds the weather well before my door, the windows they don't open. I find my strength in solitude. In being by myself alone, I harbor mine own innocence a plaque hung on the wall. There have been so numbered mornings I've woken up indoors. I am not sure of much but it seems, as if for days. Of or how I arrived, I am still not truly clear. Then given one more meal, I am shown politely to the door.

All is not a fantasy, so it may be real, somewhere in the middle on a beach somewhere near the amusement park. A boardwalk I can phantom, underneath to rest. On the better days I lay out on the beach. Most days in the world, in all reality, I am in bed by nine, up to work by six. While have encompassed much, the game, yet the game goes on.

Somewhere Some of the Time

Somewhere far and just as wide
There three wise men set
On a bank of clouds
Talking about it yet
The first one states ironically
I truly should have known
The second does agree in silence
Within a nudging glass
The one states inequitably
But it don't look like me
Then says number one
Why'd we do her in
There you have it says the second
Me neither never did
From all the laughter came as thunderous a roar
I was slated third but got to go in first
Laugh she does, for cry she would
Not realizing she means me
She's howling at my willy
There atween me knees
If you did her in then says number two
Cause she still was laughing when I came through the door
Me too says number three
Her feet still in the air they was
The what we doin here says one
Don't know realy then says two
Well now you make me wonder
That you went and mentioned it
She was the Sheririff's wife

Story Seventeen

As a child I perceived, so then I the adult in the making had experience to draw.

A native culture, may in fact not always have been that. In all permeable likelihood having migrated from another locale. Clearly, unequivocally without external intervention the longer the peoples thrived, so stayed. Aided in the comfort of so few in luxury. Redundancy in tales, became the history.

Customs expectedly become solidified to similar in base, are arrived at then steadily maintained. Of course in probability the process in is snatched. Out of the hands of reputes that may have over stayed. Thus in the pockets, off the backs of the auditioning. The planning to the carrying out, by the community in hole.

Rituals seemingly arrived at per these values may then vary within a range of said extremes. Sacrifices have been made to vary large to small, in the real imagined as trophies line the hallowed halls. In regards a thirst for hunger a quenching not arrived. Appearing absent only in the lacking of the communities desire.

Legends passed down in certain circles allege that, in what are now the North and South American continents rituals, ceremonies, possibly celebrations may have been performed with the aid of an organic material. Material known of an organic origin or nature were used by some to induce a hallucinating journey of sorts. It has been said that those in curiosity may have been seeking or attempting to satisfy a desire in reaching a higher state of consciousness, as I term it in today's fashion a recreational buzz.

Not having been my preferred method of avoiding reality. My experience in the field of traveling while never having to leave the room was, well limited. Why would any individual intentionally place themselves in a situation, knowing in advance that any reality at all could be cloaked in a disguise. With so many variables arriving on one's mind at any instant, results being dealt with reasonably must be an indescribable experience. I must confess to having witnessed a few, a small handful, in controlled experiences of sorts.

One sunny Summer day an opportunity presented itself, who was I to stand as an obstruction in the path of fate? One of these like, aforementioned people came to my attention in the form of an introduction. My daily routine at times involved interaction with customers. This was no less true on this given day. For developing a listing of different scenarios encountered, a strong similarity to a phone directory could be applied in the process. Stories were legendary among my small group of fellow employees and I was no less a contributor than any other. We will include those portions suitable in a future telling of fictitious tales.

As chance would present itself I came upon a customer, seemingly alert, responsible, and outgoing. This gent was about thirty, while cordial and polite. In a year's time on the job I had not encountered him being home. For good reason this was, he had recently obtained an experience of embarking on unemployment. Happenings as these are rare, grateful I am that they are. In this situation of lifestyle change, some people tend to unwittingly take on a bulge in their character. An alteration totally understandable with a marginal degree in sympathy. This however, will not and does not suggest that we subject ourselves to a predicament as such. After all, it could be contagious. A limit is typically set automatically, like a timer on a stove. The predetermined value is detected as opposed to length of time to be invested. In other words, the applicable length of time to complete conversation and how close to the end of the day are we.

During the course of what was left of my day, I registered and immediately purged a great deal of data. I was at first taken to the extreme concentration of my able toleration. At that point it occurred to me like a tree falling on me in the forest. I heard it though no one else did. Having not taken into consideration my own appearance, it was a true awakening as to why people approached me in an assortment of ways. After all, I did laugh briefly and out loud when an old timer asked me if I had been posing for holy pictures.

I looked up at my most recent acquaintance, about a half hour into our conversation it all became drastically clear. He was somewhat of what we still referred to as Hippies. We had reached common ground before I ever said a word.

Making my apologies, I turned heading for the door.

From time to time during course of our lifetimes we meet those that will profess the ultimate experience of any given topic. They will in fact, so to speak, uncover tales of those that which shall bring a listener's imagination to life.

This was no less likely to happen than on this given day. While I may have decidedly headed for the door with every intention of leaving, I was so sadly mistaken.

As it was explained to me in the truest sense of desperation, there would be a gathering in the very house I was standing in the coming weekend. Was it my lucky day or what? Judge me as you will but, okay judge away. I listened to the amenities that would be available accompanied by apologies for those that would not. I stood intrigued for a very brief moment when he mentioned psychedelics would be available during the earlier hours of the gathering. Joking to myself as I walked from the house how I would have to upgrade from gathering to party.

In a final curtain call without making any promises, I completed my days work and with the utmost enthusiasm addressed priority one. A cold beer or so.

In my own life as I remember, there is a strong recollection self-illumination allowing my spirit to soar at or near quitting time. This was never more assuredly guaranteed than on Fridays. Each degree of the compass became cause for a toast with one draft beer in salute of its honor. Stupendously I celebrated weekends with no commoner's zeal. If a glass could be raised, so shall it be emptied. On occasion I would forgo the tavern or bar scene altogether. Having been to several righteous establishments thus far in the week. I believe I met all obligations both socially and in adventure by Wednesday mornings. Instilled in me at birth being an insatiable sense of desire of the most incredible and absurd, who ever knew what waited just around the corner. I surely never, if avoidable dwelled into predicting what lurked in my or of anyone's future. For the sake of argument alone, is there not plenty and enough written on the walls already?

I had developed a nagging desire, regardless of the day of the week it had to be reckoned with.

Almost immediately upon receiving the coming weeks invitation, a close friend came to mind. This friend shared similarity in philosophy. For example, if it could be bottled, poured or spilled, ultimately it could or should be drank. For the remaining categories use your own vivid imaginations. Most of all, last but not least, this friend being just less than a decade older than myself was a free spirited flower child, yes a hippie. His stories from the seventies pasted to his appearance alone made him a prime candidate to attend the weekends festivities. From the very day I met this child of the '70s I have heard once if not a hundred times of his psychedelic holidays. It was time to get the two veterans of the '70s together. Let they themselves give witness to the level of satisfaction they derive from the journey. I felt compelled in extending an invitation to my near and dear and so trusted friend. His response was to say the least affirmative. Now realizing that I was going to be exposed to an unfamiliar situation with two people that I myself had never observed in this scenario. We agreed on arrangements; I would meet at my friend's house and he would drive he and I to the point of launch.

As luck would have it, I was the passenger. By mid afternoon we pulled the car onto a side street, alongside the modest home where the day's function would take place. Our host answered the door almost immediately following the first knock. I made the appropriate introductions and we sat down at the dining room table. We had walked in while party preparation was still in full swing. The host had a lady friend assisting him with the incidentals. Idle chit chat escalated at a constant yet thorough tempo. Within moments stories of survival were dominating the conversation. One story topped the next in magnitude and wild and zany episodes. For most of the day to just before dusk there were no more than twenty people occupying the house overall at any given time.

The entire group excluding only me were entranced by these live recordings of a well-liked publicized band. I personally did not care for the music but found myself intrigued by the caliber and quality of the recordings. For literally hours ten to fifteen people shared and critiqued the tapes they had recorded at live shows. Evidently only one known band permitted such a practice. Fans would travel within marginal limits almost anywhere to catch a performance.

I noticed out of the corner of my eye our host getting a little spooky. The best way I could find to describe his facial expression. There seemed to be a great level of concern on his face. Before I knew I was being coerced into the kitchen, it was explained to me that my friend and companion for the day was coming off a bit whacked out. This behavior in fact was making the host very nervous. There not being an exit strategy available in the coming moments I did my best to calm the situation. Ensuring anyone that would listen that all would me alright. With that, those that were not privy to the situation became somewhat agitated. At that point four maybe five people left.

As aware as I could be considering the situation as a whole, I was being deprived of the intensity of the journey. In failing to recall the last time I had encountered the person responsible for driving me home, my concern launched.

On some extraordinary interplanetary plane two of four crew members were being rendered helpless by the Sun's intense radiation. In other words, melt downs were about to start. Encountering our host with tears in his eyes with extended arms and hands in the air stirred my everything. Near as I was able to determine my ride had left without me. My sense of urgency leveled off as I went through the front door way and made my way to the cars last known location. I located the car, it was running with the driver not readily in sight. Just when I was ready to abandon the search, there was my friend for now chatting with some people in a pickup truck. Evidently, he was hitching a ride, I assumed this because he climbed in the passenger side door and away they went.

Returning to the car I shut off the ignition though I was unable to remove the key. I secured it the best I could and started back to the house.

As I approached the house I had a strange unexplainable feeling pass over me. The house was exactly how I left it, except for one very distinctive detail. Lights were on, music was playing, TV was on but there was no one there. I checked and rechecked every room in the including attic and basement. I was gone maybe fifteen minutes; all logic was set aside for obvious reasons. I did not dare knock on the neighbor's door while not knowing what had transpired. My best guess in making a decision was to turn off everything, leave a couple lights on, close all the doors. Sit on the couch, what will be, will be.

There was no one absolutely, not a hide nor a hair. I found stranger I thought in all reality. I sat down and sought out comfort so indiscriminately. Before I knew the goings on, I was fast asleep.

Shall let, the prophet prophesize.
In let the poet rhyme
So let the writer write
The magician for one's eyes
Upon thine own and earthen floor
I set my feet to dance
The drum will echo, the pipes alive
Bring the victor, leave the spoils
The skins for wearing, shield from the cold
Her bodies warmth comes captive
In, four walls hold the roof
A beginning to an end
Shall then let, the beggar beg
In let the baker bake
So, let the candle maker
The one, to light the wick
Shall let, admiration tear the heart
In let envy line the pockets
So, let not yours and mine alone
The barker, spins the wheel
To, the arrows point the fortune
As the troubadour, seeks the song in rhyme
While the storyteller spreads
The legends out of time

I'll not have a dream as yours
You'll not have a dream as mine
The orchard reaches many, in so occupied
I will sense the rain is coming
In a drizzle pay no mind
   I do now feel, right to my marrow in a passing still was time. Under varied trees been me, Just whispering love songs. For I, there on a good day shall be humming, when I've misplaced the words.

Story Eighteen

I maintain a fondness for the belief system. If man or woman can sustain a strong, undeniable belief someone or something it is considered in existence, therefore real.

Dreams come in yet as many forms as the insurmountable multitudes that experience them. Often, from my understanding dreams can portray such a parallel course that we feverishly become locked into a challenge of reason. I find myself during the dream experience reaching for the on/off switch to validate the fact that I am in fact dreaming. I am rarely, as far as I recall, ever confronted with a dream that I need an immediate escape route.

In life's unmistakable ride along the guard rail we have episodes. The events in which we take shovel in hand and release into the wide cavernous depths of our subconscious.

These episodes lay waiting in a covering of more recent thoughts awaiting their own primordial send off.

Confusion comes into the grand scheme of the potentially picturesque landscape that is our minds when these the real and the not so intersect.

For instance, waking up from a dream while still imagining particles or continuation of another dream or thought. As I explain this to myself, imagine looking into a mirror as a mirror behind me reflects back into the first mirror. In theory as I perceive the reflections are infinitely a link in the proverbial chain of life. Simply put, imagine our dreams as being mounted on individual mirrors, repeatedly reflecting potential thoughts or dreams in our mind. Further imagine if you will, that we have some arbitrary ability to stop a reflection at will in order to recall a memory. Imagine, regardless of how old or recent, we can stop at any given point and ponder the memory. I believe that we can master control of this type of event. There simply needs one to be focused enough to fast forward, rewind, pause and the like. What we may very well need is memorization instead of reworking training and education. If we've been here before as those in some circles suggest, we may very well be here again.

May this likely account for the parallel thoughts to be and sought in our universe? Do we travel In and out of each and every other's dreams, in so same with reality?

Like It Don't Matter

There will be differences along the way
I'd struck out, once again
If I could, just see the ball
Before it goes on by
To hear it's in the catcher's mitt
as I start my swing
One, then two, so then the third
I took a cut at each
In right field, I'd make the call
In my glove, it went
On the ground it'd go
Bout drove the old guy crazy
Coaching his last son
What a season he did have
O and 8, ain't we just great
I'll say it once again
We all deserving trophies
But together we got none
There will be differences along the way
A foul ball or home run

Park or Dock

I awakened all too easily
A moment I did stare
Beyond, above illusion
All sacred I did care
I knew to just go fishing
Time to prep the boat
A last, my loving lady
My first mate at hand
We'll need food and beer to bring
I recall, thinking oddly
How simple can she be?
Still in her pajamas
Who will make the sandwiches?
The cooler won't carry itself
I guess, if this keeps up
I'll need to buy and gas the boat
Retirements been easy
We really have good times
I, in going fishing
Can't interest her in much
Across the path, out to the dock
My boat, not yet in view
Where did I dock it, this time?
I don't recall, at last
It all comes into view
My boat is where my car should be
Laid sideways on the ground
What happened to the trailer
Where the hell's my car?

By much investigation
Plus, heralded insults
Masqueraded clues
Then the tied went out
I wondered in astonishment
My findings brought to light
There sat my car amazingly
With trailer still attached
You may find this funny
As sure my wife had done
I amused for moments
As this story not yet done
I pondered for a minute
Ate one sandwich, drank four beers
How could this have happened
We don't have a lift or ramp

In Search of Order

I have decided on "My Search of Order" as a book title for this work. For the covers, I see a sunset draped around the front and back covers. I will gladly supply the picture that I see serving this purpose. My Bio which I had sent to the Literary agent some time before now; funny aren't I. It just seems that I get side tracked and forget what I meant but not always what I said. Anyway, I believe the Bio instills a little curiosity though I am truly looking for intrigue. Anyway, back to how I came up with the title.

The complete title story will eventually come out in print, if not in this book surely another. The other night, I was at my favorite beach haunt somewhere in Maryland. I am only able to tell bits and pieces, so don't get all bent out of the shape when I leave out details.

One night, I was perched in my finest beach chair, gazing into the sunset reflecting on the water from the sky. Most of us aged beachcombers are relics from the 1960s and '70s. Many who occupy the cottages for the summer months are old Hippies. This group is further reduced by the artists. There included art school graduates, musicians, and a slim vestige of where I portray my talent in words. Strongly I recommend reading my bio. It will be here somewhere when the editing comes to a halt. I am about finished here. Anyway, I find myself this Saturday night seeking comfort from a modest wood fire. Not that I was uncomfortable by any thermal standard. The beech and the surrounding acreage are notorious for bugs.

Soon, I was entering a calm, relaxing discussion in subtleties of the horizon as the sun exchanged its rays for the shadowing of the moon. Then out of the clear blue, without any notification, nearly traumatized was I. My friend by way of recent acquaintance turned to me. Standing right across the flame from me, he asked, "So, how is the book going? Are you finished, nearly finished, or a long way off?"

"Well," said I, "I am done the text itself."

"What then is the delay, my good man?" he said with a tone worthy of interrogation.

"I have to put the individual portions of the book in the order I best see as entertaining. I am waiting for the discharge of suggestions I am to pick from. I am anticipating a bigger challenge than I have already created for myself. And then it came."

"You enjoy playing on words. You've said it yourself, countless of times."

"You're quite right," I agreed in amicable equation.

"Then how about 'My Search of Order'?"

So there we are, a title that makes limited sense while lending a sense to intrigue. All on a play of words I blurted out, couldn't have been better if it was a metaphor.

About the Author

Isaac Delagrue, born of a working-class family in a suburb of Philadelphia, is ranking high among those that dreamt to dream and not to think. He is waning for the day when a yearning to create would be permitted to surface. In many ways, he is a rebel although still a child of peace by God.

In one eradicating flash brought to light what was deemed erroneous but not to be so. Many points of challenge were to bring him only closer to an unexpected destination. It being not to reach and hold or harness yet to appreciate the gift.

CPSIA information can be obtained
at www.ICGtesting.com
Printed in the USA
BVHW03s0126181018
530388BV00003B/20/P